Pebb

T0084920

Some Kids Have Autism

by Martha E. H. Rustad

Consulting Editor: Gail Saunders-Smith, PhD

Consultant: Jennifer Repella, Director of Information
& Referral, Autism Society of America

Capstone
press

Mankato, Minnesota

Pebble Books are published by Capstone Press,
1710 Roe Crest Drive, North Mankato, Minnesota 56003.
www.capstonepress.com

Library of Congress Cataloging-in-Publication Data
Rustad, Martha E. H. (Martha Elizabeth Hillman), 1975–
    Some kids have autism / by Martha E. H. Rustad.
    p. cm. — (Pebble Books. Understanding differences) Includes
    bibliographical references and index.
    ISBN: 978-1-4296-1230-2 (hardcover)
    ISBN 978-1-4296-1772-7 (softcover pbk.)
    1. Autism in children — Juvenile literature. I. Title. II. Series.
RJ506.A9R87 2008
618.92'85882 — dc22   2007032374

Summary: Simple text and photographs describe children with autism,
    their challenges and adaptations, and their everyday activities.

Note to Parents and Teachers

The Understanding Differences set supports national social studies
standards related to individual development and identity. This book
describes children with autism and illustrates their special needs.
The photographs support early readers in understanding the text.
The repetition of words and phrases helps early readers learn new
words. This book also introduces early readers to subject-specific
vocabulary words, which are defined in the Glossary. Early readers
may need assistance to read some words and to use the Table of
Contents, Glossary, Read More, Internet Sites, and Index sections
of the book.

Printed in the United States   5787

Table of Contents

My name is.

What Is Autism?

Some kids have autism.
They have trouble
communicating.
They might point to pictures
instead of speaking.

Kids with autism might not always understand how other people feel. They might not know what a smile means.

Kids with autism sometimes like to be alone.
Kids with autism might have trouble making friends.

Kids with autism do some actions over and over. They might rock back and forth. They might repeat words.

Everyday Life

Kids with autism might have stronger senses than other kids. Bright sunlight might hurt their eyes.

Kids with autism
go to school.
Some get help
from tutors.

Kids with autism like to
have the same routine
every day.
They like to know
what will happen next.

Some kids with autism have special talents. They might be better than other kids at music, math, or other skills.

Kids with autism sometimes like to play with their friends. Their friends can help them by being patient.

Glossary

autism — a condition that causes people to have trouble communicating and forming relationships with people

communicate — to share information, ideas, or feelings with another person

patient — able to wait without becoming annoyed or angry

routine — a set order of actions or events

sense — one of the body's five ways of learning about the world; the five senses are taste, smell, touch, sight, and hearing.

tutor — a teacher that helps one student at a time

Read More

Baldwin, Carol. *Autism.* Health Matters. Chicago: Heinemann Library, 2003.

Frender, Sam, and Robin Schiffmiller. *Brotherly Feelings: Me, My Emotions, and My Brother with Asperger's Syndrome.* London: Jessica Kingsley, 2007.

Internet Sites

FactHound offers a safe, fun way to find Internet sites related to this book. All of the sites on FactHound have been researched by our staff.

Here's how:

1. Visit *www.facthound.com*

2. Choose your grade level.

3. Type in this book ID **1429612304** for age-appropriate sites. You may also browse subjects by clicking on letters, or by clicking on pictures and words.

4. Click on the **Fetch It** button.

FactHound will fetch the best sites for you!

Index

Word Count: 154
Early-Intervention Level: 20

Editorial Credits
Erika L. Shores, editor; Kim Brown, book designer

Photo Credits
All photos by Capstone Press/Karon Dubke, except cover by EyeWire (Photodisc)